SPOT 50
Garden
Birds

Camilla de la Bedoyere

Miles
KeLLY

First published in 2010 by Miles Kelly Publishing Ltd
Harding's Barn, Bardfield End Green, Thaxted, Essex, CM6 3PX, UK

Copyright © Miles Kelly Publishing Ltd 2010

This edition printed in 2013

2 4 6 8 10 9 7 5 3

Publishing Director Belinda Gallagher
Creative Director Jo Cowan
Editor Sarah Parkin
Production Manager Elizabeth Collins
Reprographics Stephan Davis, Jennifer Hunt
Assets Lorraine King

ISBN 978-1-84810-601-7

Printed in China

British Library Cataloguing-in-Publication Data
A catalogue record for this book is available from the British Library

ACKNOWLEDGEMENTS
All images are from the Miles Kelly Archives

Made with paper from a sustainable forest

www.mileskelly.net info@mileskelly.net

www.factsforprojects.com

CONTENTS

Tick the circles when you have spotted the species.

ATTRACTING BIRDS

Although birds need shrubs and trees to nest in, they will visit small gardens for food. During winter, when food is scarce, seeds and nuts put out on a bird table or in a bird feeder will attract birds into a garden. Birds also need extra food in spring, when adults are feeding their chicks.

Nests

Finding a place to build a nest is difficult for birds. Put a bird box in a tree to encourage nesting there. You can buy, or make, a bird box. Ask for an adult's help.

Leave out nesting materials, such as feathers or wool, and birds may take them to build their nests.

Never disturb a nest. If an adult bird sees you near its nest, it may abandon its eggs or nestlings.

Feeding

Solid cooking fat and seeds in a yoghurt pot can be hung from trees to encourage small birds to gardens.

Drinking and bathing

Birds need to drink and they like to wash themselves. Water in a large, shallow container or a pond with shallow fringes will attract birds to bathe in a garden.

ANATOMY

Birds are vertebrates, which are animals that have backbones. They have feathers and bills (beaks). Birds' hind limbs are adapted for perching. Their front limbs are wings and most birds can fly. Young birds hatch from eggs.

The size of the bird is measured from the tip of the bill to the tip of the tail.

The wingspan is the distance from wing tip to wing tip.

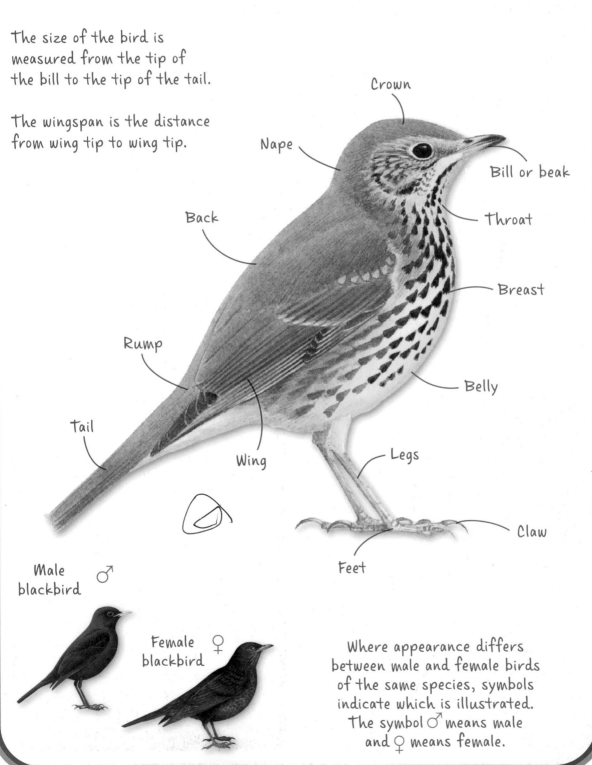

Crown

Nape

Bill or beak

Back

Throat

Breast

Rump

Belly

Tail

Wing

Legs

Claw

Feet

Male blackbird ♂

Female blackbird ♀

Where appearance differs between male and female birds of the same species, symbols indicate which is illustrated. The symbol ♂ means male and ♀ means female.

PIED WAGTAIL

Pied wagtails visit gardens, parks and open fields, often near water. They are comical birds, often seen running quickly, pausing only to look at the ground and wag their tails up and down. Although the plumage of pied wagtails is black and white, the actual patterns and depth of colour varies over the year. Females have more grey than black feathers. Pied wagtails usually eat insects.

SCALE

These birds are often mistaken for young magpies, but they can be distinguished by their wagging tails.

FACT FILE

Scientific name *Motacilla alba*

Size 17–20 cm

Wingspan 25–30 cm

Call Twittering song

Breeding 4–6 white eggs with grey spots, from April to June

Black crown, throat and upper breast

White face and black eye

White bars on wing feathers

Long tail that constantly moves

White feathers

♂

SPOTTED FLYCATCHER

Slim birds, spotted flycatchers have **grey-brown backs and pale underbodies.** Their eyes, beaks and legs are black. When they perch, spotted flycatchers flick their wings and tail. They can be found in habitats where there are trees, including gardens, parks and woodlands. These fast-flying birds catch their prey while on the wing. Damselflies and butterflies are two of their favourite prey.

SCALE

The number of spotted flycatchers has dropped dramatically in recent years and they are now a threatened species. This may be due to loss of habitat.

FACT FILE

Scientific name
Muscicapa striata

Size 13–15 cm

Wingspan 23–25 cm

Call Soft but scratchy song

Breeding 4–5 pale blue eggs, from May to June

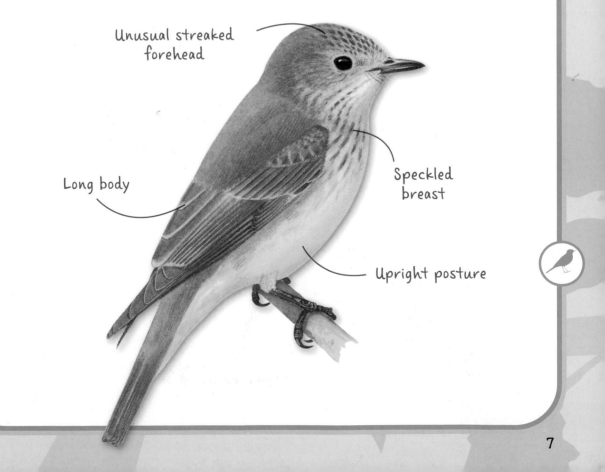

Unusual streaked forehead

Long body

Speckled breast

Upright posture

WAXWING

Pretty waxwings spend the winter in **Britain and fly north to Scandinavia to breed in the spring**. They feed on crops of berries, paticularly rowan and hawthorn, but they also eat fruit, such as apples. Waxwings sometimes travel in big flocks and keep flying south through Britain as they search for more food. They can quickly strip bushes of their berries.

These birds are most common in Scotland and in northern and eastern England.

FACT FILE

Scientific name
Bombycilla garrulus

Size 18 cm

Wingspan 32–35 cm

Call High-pitched trill, 'trreeee'

Breeding Lays up to six eggs in one brood from May to June

Large crest

Dark eye with black line through it

Small bill

Black bib on throat

Red spots on wings

Plump body

White wing bars

DUNNOCK

Dunnocks are sometimes called hedge sparrows because at first glance they look very similar to the house sparrow. However a dunnock's beak is much slimmer than a sparrow's, because it feeds on insects rather than seeds (stouter beaks are better at cracking seeds open). Male and female dunnocks look similar with brown streaking and pink legs, although the females are a little duller.

SCALE

Cuckoos lay eggs in dunnock nests. The dunnocks are unaware that they are incubating an intruder. After hatching, the cuckoo fledgling throws the dunnock chicks out of the nest.

FACT FILE

Scientific name
Prunella modularis

Size 13–15 cm

Wingspan 19–21 cm

Call Soft warble

Breeding 4–6 pale blue, glossy eggs, from April to July

Thin, sharp beak

Speckled feathers on back

Blue-grey throat, breast and eye-stripe

Pink legs

WREN

One of the smallest birds that visit gardens, wrens are small, stocky, restless birds. They can be seen rushing around, particularly under trees or bushes where they are well camouflaged. Wrens have brown backs and brown-and-cream eye stripes. Their pert tails are constantly moving. They use grass and leaves to build their globe-shaped nests in bushes, trees and holes in walls. The nests are lined with feathers.

SCALE

Wrens can travel many kilometres in search of food, or to find habitats that are sheltered from harsh weather.

FACT FILE

Scientific name
Troglodytes troglodytes

Size 9–10 cm

Wingspan 13–17 cm

Call Loud trills and warbling

Breeding 5–8 white eggs with reddish spots, from April to July

Short, upright tail

Plumage is reddish brown on back, with faint black bars

Faint eye stripe

Pale feathers underneath

Beak is very narrow and tip points slightly downwards

BLACKBIRD

Male blackbirds are unmistakeable visitors to the garden. They have all-black plumage, distinctive yellow bills and yellow rings around their eyes. Females are harder to spot as they are dull brown all over, except for a paler streak on their throats. Blackbirds can often be seen hopping along the ground, looking for food. When alarmed, they have a loud, shrill call that sounds like a 'chack-ak-chack-ak'.

SCALE

Blackbird nests are made from grasses and lined with mud. The birds often build their nests in open, exposed places where birds of prey and cats may reach them.

FACT FILE

Latin name *Turdus merula*
Size 23–30 cm
Wingspan 35–38 cm
Call Flute-like and loud
Breeding 4–5 light blue eggs with red spots, from March to April

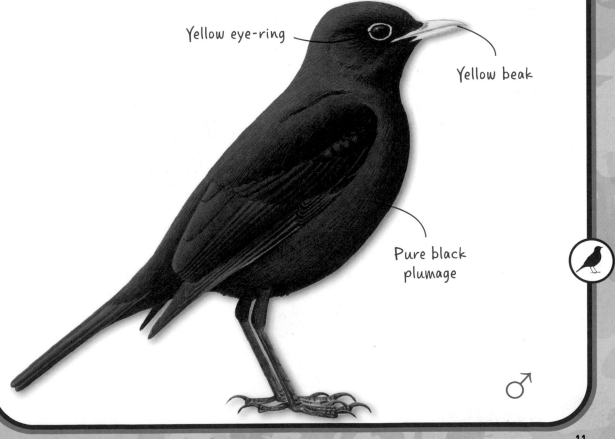

Yellow eye-ring

Yellow beak

Pure black plumage

♂

FIELDFARE

One of the largest types of thrush, fieldfares are social birds. They are often seen hopping along the ground. They visit gardens when they cannot find food in open fields and hedgerows. During autumn and winter, they can occasionally be seen eating ripe fruit that has fallen from trees. Fieldfares usually feed, fly and roost together in flocks.

SCALE

Fieldfares migrate to the UK in winter, but they spend the rest of the year in Scandinavia where they breed. Nowadays, fewer fieldfares are seen in the UK.

FACT FILE

Scientific name *Turdus pilaris*
Size 22–27 cm
Wingspan 39–42 cm
Call Loud 'chack-chack'
Breeding 5–6 eggs
from April to July

Blue-grey head

Chestnut back

Short, thin, yellow beak

Dark tail

Speckled brown breast

MISTLE THRUSH

The mistle thrush is Britain's largest thrush. It is also known as the 'stormcock', because it sings in the treetops when the wind is blowing hard. It forages on the ground for insects, worms and snails in spring and summer, and moves by bounding along in leaps. In the winter, mistle thrushes feed on fruit and berries, especially yew, hawthorn, holly, mistletoe and ivy.

SCALE

Mistle thrushes are usually shy of people, but they have been known to attack other animals, even dogs, during their breeding season.

FACT FILE

Scientific name *Turdus viscivorus*
Size 26–28 cm
Wingspan 42–48 cm
Call Loud rattling chatter 'tsarrk' or flute-like song
Breeding 3–5 eggs are laid and there are two broods a year, from March to June

Dark eye

Strong bill

Grey-brown back

Whitish breast with dark spots

Powerful, long legs

Long wings

REDWING

Redwings are most commonly seen in woods and fields, often in large flocks. They forage for worms, slugs, snails, insects and berries, sometimes in the company of fieldfares and song thrushes. Large groups may settle on one tree and stay there until they have stripped it of its berries. These birds are winter visitors to Britain, many of them travelling here from Scandinavia. They return to the continent in March, ready for the breeding season.

SCALE

Redwings travel far and wide to search for food, but they are very vulnerable to cold and a shortage of food. If there are no berries, they may die in their hundreds.

FACT FILE

Scientific name *Turdus iliacus*
Size 20–22 cm
Wingspan 33–35 cm
Call Variable songs from 'seep' to 'chuk'
Breeding 4–6 eggs are laid in each two broods from April to July

Bold white eye-stripe

Silver-white feathers on underside with speckles

Chestnut-red flanks

ROBIN

One of the most easily recognized garden birds, robins are dainty, with plump bodies and red breasts. They are known as gardeners' friends, as they often perch nearby when soil is being dug over, and quickly leap on any insects that are exposed. Males and females look similar. Robins are associated with holly berries, not only because of Christmas, but also because in winter, when food is scarce, robins feed on the berries.

SCALE

Robins do not migrate from the UK, but in winter, robins from colder countries often migrate to the UK. These birds have paler breasts and are less tame.

FACT FILE

Scientific name
Erithacus rubecula
Size 12–15 cm
Wingspan 20–22 cm
Call Warbling song
Breeding 5–6 white eggs, speckled with red, from March to July

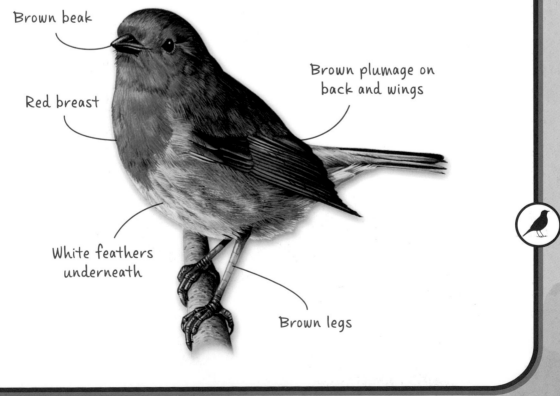

Brown beak

Red breast

Brown plumage on back and wings

White feathers underneath

Brown legs

SONG THRUSH

Often seen darting around between bushes, song thrushes use their ears and eyes to search for small insects or worms to eat. They have brown backs and pale, creamy-white speckled chests. Males and females look similar. Song thrushes live in woodlands, gardens and fields. They nest in trees, bushes and garden sheds.

SCALE

Thrushes build cup-shaped nests from grasses and twigs. The inside is lined with mud and rotting wood, and is stuck together with saliva.

FACT FILE

Scientific name
Turdus philomelos
Size 23 cm
Wingspan 33–36 cm
Call Loud, clear and flute-like
Breeding 4–6 pale blue eggs, from March to August

Large eyes

Slender bill

Brown back

Speckled, cream breast

CARRION CROW

Both male and female carrion crows have black plumage with stout black bills. A close look at their feathers reveals a blue and purple shine. These crows live in a wide range of habitats, from gardens to coasts and mountains. Males and females share the job of building a nest, which is usually sited near the top of a tree, an electricity pylon or on a cliff edge.

SCALE

Animals that feed on dead bodies are called carrion eaters. Although these crows eat carrion, they also feed on eggs, insects and grain.

FACT FILE

Scientific name *Corvus corone*
Size 44–50 cm
Wingspan 80–100 cm
Call Loud kraa-kraa
Breeding 4–6 blotchy blue-green eggs, from April to May

All over black plumage with blue sheen

Short, heavy bill with small feathers at the base

Strong, perching toes with sharp claws

JACKDAW

Small members of the crow family, jackdaws can survive in many different types of habitat and eat a wide variety of food. They usually live and roost in large groups, or colonies. They make their nests in a variety of places including rock faces, chimneys, churches and natural holes in trees. Jackdaws prey on the eggs and fledglings of woodpigeons and other birds. They also eat insects, worms and will forage on rubbish dumps.

SCALE

Rooks, carrion crows and jackdaws can easily be mistaken for one another. However these birds are quicker and more agile than most members of the crow family.

FACT FILE

Scientific name
Corvus monedula

Size 33 cm

Wingspan 65–75 cm

Call Harsh calls, 'tchak'

Breeding 4–6 pale blue eggs in April

Paler feathers on neck

White eye-ring

Black, glossy plumage

JAY

These birds are members of the crow family but, unlike most of their relatives, they have colourful plumage. Their bodies are pinky-brown and there are distinctive blue flashes on the wings. Jays are sociable birds, and males and females often stay together for life. They can copy the calls of other birds, but often make a loud screeching noise when they arrive in a garden.

SCALE

Jays feed on acorns and bury up to 3000 in one month. They sometimes forget about them, so the acorns grow into trees.

FACT FILE

Scientific name
Garrulus glandarius

Size 31–35 cm

Wingspan 54–59 cm

Call Loud and harsh screech

Breeding 3–10 pale green, speckled eggs, from April to July

Streaked crown

Pinkish-brown body

Black moustache

White flash on the rump

Blue feathers on wing

Pink legs

MAGPIE

Large black-and-white birds, magpies have very long tails. Their tails are longer than their bodies and tinged with green. Magpies are most common in rural areas, especially near farms, but they often visit gardens and parks where they feed on rubbish and scraps. In spring, magpies can come together in large flocks called 'parliaments'. They are blamed for eating the eggs and nestlings of songbirds.

SCALE

Magpies are believed to bring bad luck. However saying 'Good morning Mr Magpie' when you see one is supposed to ward off evil.

FACT FILE

Scientific name *Pica pica*

Size 41–51 cm

Wingspan 50–60 cm

Call Loud and harsh 'chacka chacka'

Breeding 5–8 glossy, spotted eggs, from April to May

Dark-coloured head

Blue-black wings

Long, greenish-black tail with rounded tip

White feathers underneath

ROOK

The rook is one of the best-known **British social birds, and lives in large flocks or colonies.** Rooks often build their nests close to one another. In the winter, the tops of trees may be home to many of these birds and their large nests. Rooks fly with a slow, flapping and gliding flight pattern. They feed on snails, larvae and grain, but may gather near roadsides to feed on animals that have been killed by vehicles.

SCALE

There are more than one million breeding pairs of rooks in Britain. However numbers dropped drastically in the 1960s because of pesticide poisoning.

FACT FILE

Scientific name
Corvus frugilegus
Size 44–46 cm
Wingspan 81–99 cm
Call Very loud raucous 'caaar'
Breeding 3–6 eggs are laid
from March to June

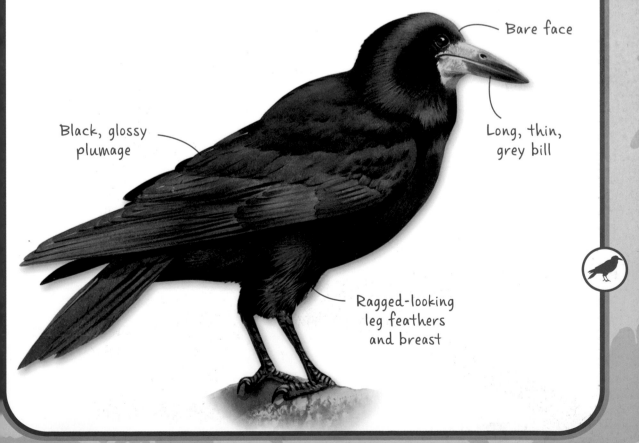

Bare face

Black, glossy
plumage

Long, thin,
grey bill

Ragged-looking
leg feathers
and breast

STARLING

These birds have a reputation as one of the noisiest visitors to the garden. This is partly because they prefer to live and feed in large groups. These flocks are an amazing sight as they swoop into parkland or circle above a garden looking for suitable perches. Starlings are medium-sized birds that hold their bodies upright, as they busily march around looking for food. Their diet includes insects, worms, seeds and scraps.

SCALE

Starlings are mimics — they can learn the songs of other birds and copy them. They don't stop at birdsong — they can also imitate car alarms and ring tones.

FACT FILE

Scientific name
Sturnus vulgaris

Size 19–22 cm

Wingspan 37–43 cm

Call Twitters, clicks and whistles

Breeding 5–7 pale blue eggs, from April to May

Slender, yellow beak

Small, light-coloured flecks on body and wings

Pointed wings

Metallic green-and-purple sheen on feathers

Short tail

♂

BLACKCAP

In the spring, the blackcap can be seen and heard singing from a high perch, often an oak tree. They often work their way through brambles and undergrowth with garden warblers. Although mainly an insect-eater, blackcaps eat berries and fruits in the autumn. Increasing numbers of blackcaps are overwintering in Britain, and visiting bird tables during winter.

SCALE

FACT FILE

Scientific name *Sylvia atricapilla*

Size 13–15 cm

Wingspan 20–23 cm

Call 'Tak' when disturbed, song is loud and warbling

Breeding Two clutches of eggs April to July and 4–5 eggs in each

Blackcaps can be quite aggressive when competing for scraps in the garden, often frightening off much larger birds.

Males have a black cap

Grey-brown upperparts

Notched tail

♂

CHIFFCHAFF

Chiffchaffs visit Britain in the summer. However in southern England and Ireland, some of them have given up migrating in the winter and manage to survive the coldest months. These little birds are hard to spot because their olive-brown plumage hides them well in the vegetation. They are likely to be found close to water. Chiffchaffs eat insects and spiders that they find amongst leaves and flowers.

SCALE

Young chiffchaffs stay in the nest for about two weeks before they are ready to fly. If any animal approaches them in the meantime, they will try to attack it.

FACT FILE

Scientific name
Phylloscopus collybita
Size 10–11 cm
Wingspan 15–21 cm
Call 'Hweet' or 'chip-chap'
Breeding 5–6 eggs laid from April to July, hatching about 14 days later

Pale stripe over eye

Olive-brown plumage on back and head

Thin, short bill

Short wingtips

Grey-white underparts

Thin, dark legs

GARDEN WARBLER

Despite their name, garden warblers prefer woodland to gardens, although they do visit gardens with mature trees. These birds are migrants and only come to the UK in summer, arriving in April and leaving in the middle of July. Their plain appearance helps to camouflage them, and they spend a lot of time in bushes and hedgerows, searching for insects and berries to eat.

SCALE

There are about 400 different types of warbler and many are dull in appearance. They are well-known for their melodious singing.

FACT FILE

Scientific name *Sylvia borin*
Size 14 cm
Wingspan 20–22 cm
Call Melodic song
Breeding 3–7 dull cream eggs with grey spots, from late May to June

Small, slender beak

Olive-brown plumage

Paler colour underneath

GOLDCREST

Europe's smallest bird, the goldcrest still **manages to migrate across the North Sea from Scandinavia to spend the winter in Britain.** The male goldcrest raises his bright crest when courting, and also when rivals stray into his territory. Their main food consists of spiders and small insects, such as aphids. Goldcrests are found in woodland, and in parks and gardens containing conifers, such as larch and fir.

SCALE

Goldcrests mingle with tits and firecrests, which are closely related, in food-hunting winter flocks.

FACT FILE

Scientific name *Regulus regulus*

Size 9 cm

Wingspan 13–16 cm

Call High-pitched 'zeek' and trill, also 'si-si-si'

Breeding Two broods April to July, 7–8 eggs in each

Greenish back

Male has distinctive golden-orange crest, with a black stripe on each side

Fine moustache streak

Round body

♂

WILLOW WARBLER

Flying in from North Africa every spring, the willow warbler is one of the most commonly seen summer visitors to Europe. On its arrival in Britain, it often feeds on insects found on flowering willows. These birds are always on the move, flicking their wings as they busily forage for insects. Willow warblers sing their songs from trees and bushes, while working their way through foliage seeking insects, and while flying.

SCALE

When courting the female, the male willow warbler perches near her and slowly waves one or both of his wings at her.

FACT FILE

Scientific name
Phylloscopus trochilus
Size 11 cm
Wingspan 17–22 cm
Call 'Hoo-id', song is a falling sequence of clear notes
Breeding One brood of 6–7 eggs from April to May

Yellow eye-stripe

Olive-brown plumage

Pale, yellowish white underparts

Pale legs

BLUE TIT

Blue tits are small, lively birds and agile movers. They can hang upside down from twigs and bird feeders while eating, and can even perch on milk bottles to peck at the top and drink the milk. Blue tits have bright blue crowns and a yellow breast, with a slight black stripe. Females lay large clutches of eggs, and have been known to lay as many as 19 eggs in a single clutch.

SCALE

Blue tits are popular because they feed on aphids. These are small insects that damage plants. They also eat other insects, including caterpillars, and nuts from feeders.

FACT FILE

Scientific name
Cyanistes caeruleus
Size 11–12 cm
Wingspan 17–20 cm
Call Clear and high-pitched
Breeding 7–12 white eggs with purplish spots, from April to May

Blue crown

Thick black
eye stripe

White cheeks

Blue wings
and tail

Yellow breast

♂

COAL TIT

The smallest member of the tit family, coal tits are far more timid than blue tits. These birds will visit bird tables, but they carry food away and hide it. Coal tits are naturally birds of the forest. They forage in trees for live prey, such as spiders and insects, and search the ground for nuts and seeds. Acrobatic birds, coal tits can be seen creeping up tree trunks. They have a preference for deep woods of conifers.

SCALE

Coal tits sometimes forage with mixed flocks of goldcrests and treecreepers through trees and bracken.

FACT FILE

Scientific name *Parus ater*

Size 11.5 cm

Wingspan 17–21 cm

Call 'Tsui' or 'tsee'

Breeding Lays up to 11 eggs in one brood April to June

White cheek and nape

Small in size

Black bib

White wing bars

GREAT TIT

The energetic and sprightly great tit is a common sight on a bird table, where it fights off other birds to get a bigger portion of food. It is the largest of all British tits, but is still very agile and acrobatic in its flying and perching skills, and can even swing upside down. Great tits have powerful bills that can be used to break tough nuts, but they can eat a wide variety of food, including insects, berries, nuts and seeds.

SCALE

Great tits originally lived in woodlands, but they have been drawn to gardens and parks by the food available in these new habitats.

FACT FILE

Scientific name *Parus major*

Size 14 cm

Wingspan 22–25 cm

Call Very varied, e.g. 'chink', 'seetoo', 'tui-tui'

Breeding Five or more eggs are laid from April

Pale blue wings

Black crown

White cheeks

Blue-grey tail with white sides

Green back and bright yellow chest

♂

LONG-TAILED TIT

Apart from its long tail, this is a tiny bird. They usually move in small flocks, seeking insects for food, and woods and hedgerows are good places to see them. These birds use their tiny beaks to harvest insects. They also feed on buds and small amounts of lichen and algae in the trees. Long-tailed tits were almost killed off by severe frosts in 1947 in Britain.

SCALE

Because of their small size, long-tailed tits are vulnerable to cold, and flock members huddle together for warmth at night.

FACT FILE

Scientific name
Aegithalos caudatus

Size 14 cm

Wingspan 16–19 cm

Call 'Zee–zee' and 'trrr'

Breeding One brood of 8–12 eggs from April to June

Bold eyebrow markings

Pink shoulder patches

Long tail

Fluffy pink-and-white plumage

Small, round body

MARSH TIT

The marsh tit is actually found in woodlands, where it hunts through the trees for insects and forages on the ground for seeds. It holds tough seeds, such as beechmast, with one foot while pecking them open with its strong beak. These birds often team up with flocks of several tit species. They appear in gardens in the winter if food is put out.

SCALE

Marsh tits do not linger at the bird table. They carry food away to eat later, and hide it in the ground or in cracks in tree bark.

FACT FILE

Scientific name *Poecile palustris*

Size 11.5 cm

Wingspan 18–19 cm

Call Shrill 'pitchu', song is 'chip, chip, chip'

Breeding 6–8 eggs, one brood April to June

Short bill

Glossy black cap

Small, black bib

NUTHATCH

Unusual looking birds, nuthatches are often seen running up and down the trunks of trees, searching for insects. They use their sharp, pointed beaks to search cracks in tree bark for bugs or seeds. Males and females look similar, but the colours are slightly darker in males. They live in woodlands, but often visit gardens in search of nuts and seeds.

SCALE

Nuthatches are easily mistaken for woodpeckers, as they both perch on the bark of trees. However nuthatches are the only birds that run headfirst down a tree.

FACT FILE

Scientific name *Sitta europaea*

Size 11–15 cm

Wingspan 20–25 cm

Call Loud piping notes

Breeding 6–9 white eggs, from April to May

Large head with very short neck

Long, black eye stripe

Orange feathers underneath

White cheeks and throat

TREECREEPER

The treecreeper is an inconspicuous little bird, but is easily recognized by its long, curving beak, which it uses to probe bark as it creeps up the tree trunk. Almost always working upwards from the bottom of the trunk, the treecreeper uses its stiff tail feathers as a support against the bark. As it creeps upwards, it spirals around the tree trunk, then flies down to the bottom of the next tree.

SCALE

The treecreeper occasionally comes into gardens, but will not usually approach the bird table. It can be fed in the garden by smearing fat onto a tree trunk.

FACT FILE

Scientific name
Certhia familiaris

Size 12.5 cm

Wingspan 18–21 cm

Call High-pitched 'tsit' or 'tsee'

Breeding One brood, 5–6 eggs
April to June

White eyebrow

Long, curved bill

Brown plumage above

Long, pointed tail

White plumage underneath

BRAMBLING

The brambling is very fond of beech woods, foraging through them in flocks sometimes numbering thousands. When beechmast crops fail, or when the weather is particularly harsh, bramblings are attracted to gardens where food has been put out. These birds often move in mixed flocks containing chaffinches and other finches, as they hunt for insects and seeds on the woodland floor.

SCALE

Bramblings are ground feeders, and they usually take the seeds and other scraps dropped from the bird table by other birds.

FACT FILE

Scientific name
Fringilla montifringilla
Size 14.5 cm
Wingspan 25–28 cm
Call 'Kvek' when flying, single 'dzwee' song
Breeding One brood of 5–7 eggs May to June

Black head and back with scaling in winter

White rump

Bright orange plumage

White belly

♂

BULLFINCH

Bullfinches are often seen in couples, **and are thought to pair for life.** They are shy and secretive birds, and like to stay close to cover. The bullfinch rarely forages on the ground, and is usually spotted in trees and bushes, using its strong beak to harvest seeds, berries and buds. In autumn and early winter these birds feed on seeds, such as ash keys.

SCALE

Bullfinches are rare at the bird table, but they will take shelled peanuts from a net.

FACT FILE

Scientific name
Pyrrhula pyrrhula
Size 15 cm
Wingspan 22–26 cm
Call Distinct, low, piping 'phew'
Breeding Two broods, 4–5 eggs
April to June

Black cap

Stubby, black bill

White rump

Rosy red breast

♂

CHAFFINCH

Male chaffinches have rosy pink breasts and cheeks with bluish-grey heads. Females have greenish-brown backs and greyish-brown feathers underneath. Chaffinches have melodic songs, which differ from one region to another. They eat fruit, insects and seeds that they find on the ground, but they also catch insects in flight.

SCALE

Chaffinches build their cup-shaped nests with grasses, mosses and lichens in the fork of a tree. The nests are lined with feathers and joined with spiders' webs.

FACT FILE

Scientific name *Fringilla coelebs*

Size 14–16 cm

Wingspan 24–28 cm

Call Loud trills and short 'pink'

Breeding 2–8 light blue eggs in April, incubated for 11–13 days

Grey feathers on head

Bands of white on wings

Pink chest feathers

Brown tail

♂

GOLDFINCH

Distinctive visitors to the garden, goldfinches are easy to identify. Males and females look alike – they have red faces with white cheeks and throats. The top of the head is black, and the wings have broad yellow bands. In winter, many goldfinches migrate south to warmer weather, returning in March and April, but some stay in the UK all year round.

SCALE

It was once fashionable to have caged birds in the home, and goldfinches were a favourite because of their melodious song.

FACT FILE

Scientific name
Carduelis carduelis

Size 12 cm

Wingspan 21–25 cm

Call Soft twills and twitters

Breeding 4–7 speckled blue eggs, from May to August

Brown back

Pinkish beak

Red, black and white face

White feathers underneath

Golden bars on black-and-brown wings

GREENFINCH

Greenfinches are stout birds that often live in groups, in hedges and other dense vegetation. Their bodies are mostly green, with yellow bands on their wings. Females and males look similar, but the females have more brown in their plumage. Greenfinches often come together in groups, or colonies, at breeding time. When the juveniles have left the nest, greenfinches may travel south for the winter.

SCALE

These birds are common in gardens, where they can find food easily. They like peanuts and sunflower seeds in particular.

FACT FILE

Scientific name *Carduelis chloris*

Size 15 cm

Wingspan 25–28 cm

Call Wheezy song with whistles and twitters

Breeding 4–6 speckled cream eggs, from April to May

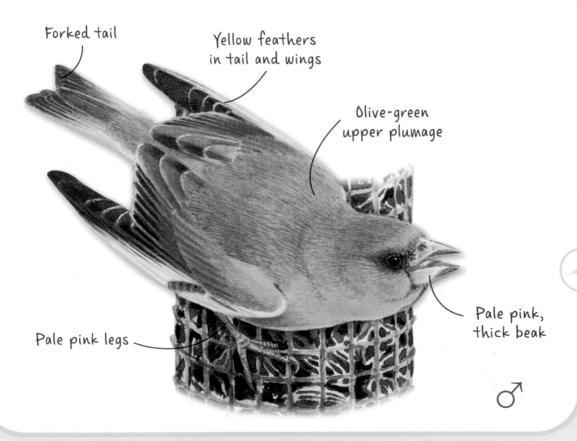

Forked tail

Yellow feathers in tail and wings

Olive-green upper plumage

Pale pink legs

Pale pink, thick beak

♂

SISKIN

Siskins are commonly found in conifer woods. Their numbers have grown in recent years because of the increase of conifer plantations around Britain. They have spread further south and can now be found all across the country throughout the year. During the winter, siskins often gather in large flocks, sometimes in the company of redpolls, which are a type of small finch.

SCALE

Siskins love seeds, but they will visit gardens where they can find regular supplies of shelled peanuts. They also love the seeds of alder and birch trees.

FACT FILE

Scientific name *Carduelis spinus*

Size 11–13 cm

Wingspan 20–23 cm

Call Clear 'tsu-ee' or rapid trills

Breeding 4–5 eggs are laid in one or two broods from May to July

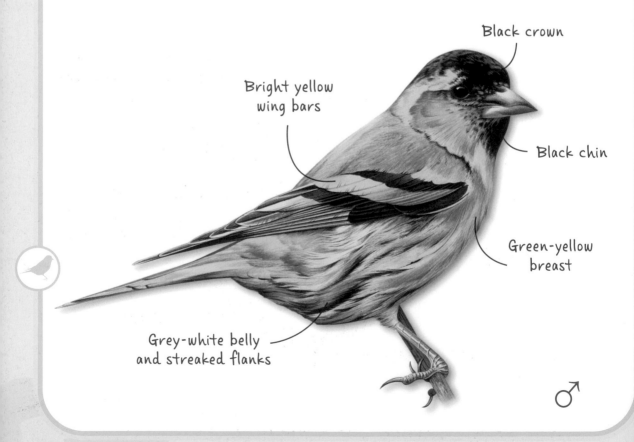

Black crown

Bright yellow wing bars

Black chin

Green-yellow breast

Grey-white belly and streaked flanks

♂

HOUSE SPARROW

Small, active birds, sparrows are a familiar sight in the garden. Males have grey caps and chests, and a bold black patch on the throat and upper chest. They also have a black eye stripe. Females are much duller in colour with a chestnut-coloured stripe over their eyes. Sparrows' nests are made from straw and grasses, and are lined with feathers.

SCALE

The house sparrow is becoming increasingly rare and has disappeared from some parts of the UK. No one knows for sure why their numbers are falling.

FACT FILE

Scientific name *Passer domesticus*

Size 14–15 cm

Wingspan 20–25 cm

Call Chirps

Breeding 3–5 pale blue eggs with grey blotches, from April to June

Yellow-brown beak in winter (black in summer)

Grey cap

Chestnut brown plumage on back is darkly streaked

Black throat patch and eye stripe

Grey breast

Pale brown legs

♂

REED BUNTING

The reed bunting is a bird of the wetlands. However it has now spread into some drier habitats. In the winter, it leaves its reed beds and marshes, and moves to the fields. Here it hunts for seeds and insects alongside finches and other buntings. If threatened by approaching danger, the reed bunting pretends to be injured, crawling along with wings half spread, leading the threat away from its nest.

SCALE

Reed buntings are primarily ground feeders, so are in danger of starvation when there is a covering of snow. They increasingly visit gardens in the winter for food.

FACT FILE

Scientific name
Emberiza schoeniclus
Size 15.5 cm
Wingspan 21–26 cm
Call Loud 'tseek' and metallic 'chink'
Breeding Two broods, 4–5 eggs in each, April to June

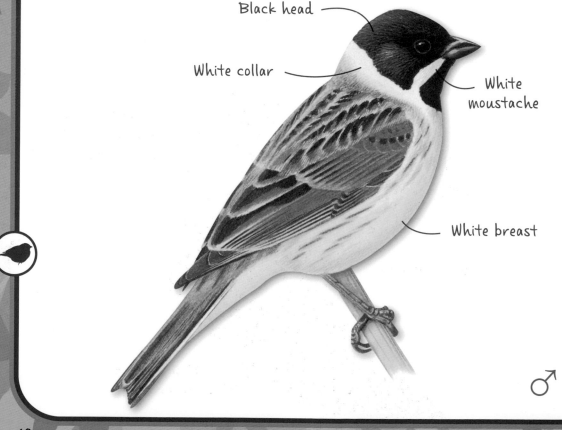

Black head

White collar

White moustache

White breast

♂

HOUSE MARTIN

Often mistaken for swallows, house martins are actually smaller, have shorter tail forks and a white chin. They feed on flying insects, swooping over water or farmland to catch their prey. House martins are rarely seen on land, although they may be spotted over the garden at dusk. They often live in gardens with muddy pools, since they make their nests from mud. These summer birds migrate to warm countries in October, returning in spring.

SCALE

House martins are occasionally attracted to hot air balloons. They fly in circles above the balloons, maybe enjoying a free ride on the rising current of warm air.

FACT FILE

Scientific name *Delichon urbica*

Size 12–15 cm

Wingspan 25–30 cm

Call Twittering

Breeding 4–5 white eggs, from May to August

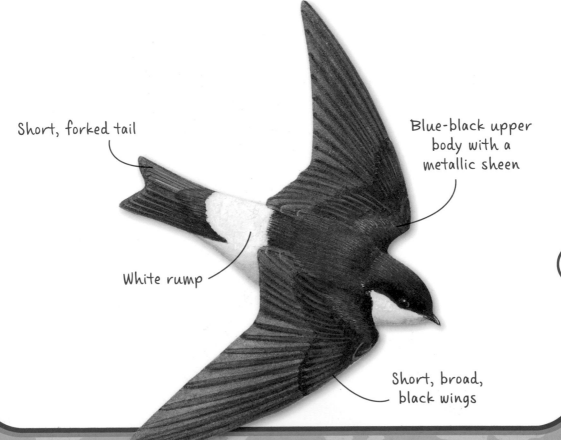

Short, forked tail

Blue-black upper body with a metallic sheen

White rump

Short, broad, black wings

SWALLOW

Difficult to identify because they are rarely seen near the ground, swallows are extremely agile flyers. They can be seen swooping through the air as they hunt for insects to eat. Their wings are long and pointed, and their tails are deeply forked, unlike swifts and house martins. Swallows migrate to Europe from Africa in spring. Fewer swallows are coming to the UK than previously, but the reason for this is unknown.

SCALE

Farmers avoid destroying swallow nests because the birds are thought to bring good luck. Swallows use second-hand nests — some are more than 50 years old.

FACT FILE

Scientific name *Hirundo rustica*

Size 17–22 cm

Wingspan 30–35 cm

Call Rapid twitter

Breeding 4–5 eggs with white spots, from April to August

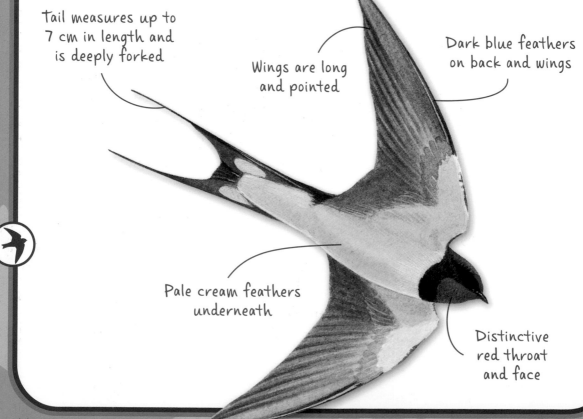

Tail measures up to 7 cm in length and is deeply forked

Wings are long and pointed

Dark blue feathers on back and wings

Pale cream feathers underneath

Distinctive red throat and face

SWIFT

Swifts are extraordinary birds and superb fliers. They rarely come to land and spend almost all of their lives in the air, even sleeping while in flight. Once fledglings leave the nest, they may remain airborne for the next two or three years, until they reach breeding age. Swifts feed on insects and spiders that they catch in mid-air. They arrive in Britain in April, for the breeding season, and often nest in the eaves of old buildings. They leave in July or August.

SCALE

British swifts spend the winter in Africa, where they follow the rains. After rainfall, insect populations boom, providing a good food supply for these birds.

FACT FILE

Scientific name *Apus apus*

Size 16–17 cm

Wingspan 42–48 cm

Call Loud screeches and screams

Breeding 2–3 eggs are laid from May to June

Plumage is black-brown all over

Long, narrow wings

Deeply forked, short tail

GREAT SPOTTED WOODPECKER

Boldly coloured, great spotted woodpeckers are black and white with red under the tail. Males also have a red splash on the nape of the neck. Youngsters look similar, but the colours are less bold. These birds are the size of a blackbird. They live in woodlands, parks and gardens with large trees, and scurry across tree trunks looking for insects to eat.

SCALE

Woodpeckers make a characteristic drumming noise with their beaks on trees. They look for bugs in the cracks in bark, and have very long tongues for picking up food.

FACT FILE

Scientific name
Dendrocopos major

Size 22–33 cm

Wingspan 34–42 cm

Call Sharp, short 'tchak'

Breeding 4–7 white eggs, from April to June

Pointed beak

Red nape of neck

White wing patches

Red under the tail

GREEN WOODPECKER

The handsome green woodpecker lives in woodlands and parklands, and is Britain's largest woodpecker. It uses its long, pointed beak to excavate its nest hole and to dig for ants, its main food. The ants stick to the woodpecker's long, sticky tongue. In the garden, these birds are more likely to drill the lawn for ants than approach the bird table. When ants' nests are frozen, woodpeckers have been known to bore into beehives.

SCALE

Green woodpeckers are shy but noisy birds, and are unmistakable with their bold colouring. Also unmistakable is its loud cry, resembling hysterical laughter.

FACT FILE

Scientific name *Picus viridis*

Size 30–33 cm

Wingspan 40–42 cm

Call Loud, laughing 'gluck-gluck-gluck'

Breeding 5–7 eggs, one brood May to July

Crimson-red crown and nape

Black-and-red moustache

Bright green upperparts

Green-grey underparts

♂

LESSER SPOTTED WOODPECKER

The lesser spotted woodpecker is about the size of a sparrow. Its colouring is like the greater spotted woodpecker's, but arranged differently. It is a shy bird, hunting insects out of sight in high branches. Lesser spotted woodpeckers drum to mark their territory. They are hardly ever seen at the bird table, approaching it very nervously if at all. These birds are normally only seen in England and Wales.

SCALE

Unlike other woodpeckers, lesser spotted woodpeckers join winter feeding flocks of mixed tits.

FACT FILE

Scientific name
Dendrocopus minor

Size 13–14 cm

Wingspan 25–27 cm

Call 'Kee-kee-kee', weak 'tchik'

Breeding 4–6 eggs, one brood
May to July

Bright red crown

Black-and-white feathers

Short, thin, grey bill

♂

COLLARED DOVE

The collared dove has become common in Britain only in the last 50 years, having migrated from India via Europe. This bird stays close to human society. It feeds alongside farm poultry and cattle, sharing their meals, and also hangs around docks, breweries, stables and zoos, where there is grain to be found. It is seen in both towns and villages, and soon locates local bird tables, turning up regularly for seeds and scraps.

SCALE

Where food is plentiful, the collared dove may feed in sizable flocks, especially in winter. It eats snails and insects as well as seeds.

FACT FILE

Scientific name
Streptopelia decaocto
Size 28–32 cm
Wingspan 47–55 cm
Call Deep 'coo-coooo, coo', 'hwee' in flight
Breeding Two eggs, 2–3 broods all year

Narrow black half-collar

Pinkish breast

Fawny grey wings

White undertail

FERAL PIGEON

Seen everywhere from wheat fields to city squares, the feral pigeon is descended from the rock dove. Specially bred to provide food and birds for racing, it then reverted to the wild. It has interbred widely, and has a large variety of colours and markings. Feral pigeons colonize all human environments. They nest on ledges and feed on whatever can be found. These birds also feed in flocks in the countryside.

SCALE

The wild rock dove is now found only along the rocky coasts of northern and western Scotland and on the coasts of Northern Ireland.

FACT FILE

Scientific name *Columba livia*

Size 31–34 cm

Wingspan 63–70 cm

Call 'Ruh-ruh-ruh'

Breeding Two eggs, three broods, breeds all year

Black-and-white bill

Dark wing bars

White rump

Blue-grey plumage

Short, pink legs

STOCK DOVE

More solitary than woodpigeons, stock doves can sometimes be seen feeding alongside them in winter. Found everywhere in Britain except the extreme north of Scotland, the stock dove's habitats include woods, rocky coasts, dunes, cliffs and parkland. It occasionally eats snails and larvae, but most of its food is vegetable, including leaves, crops such as beans and corn, clover, seeds, buds and flowers.

SCALE

The stock dove has an impressive display in the breeding season. Both males and females fly around in circles, gliding with raised wings, and 'clapping' their wings.

FACT FILE

Scientific name *Columba oenas*

Size 32–34 cm

Wingspan 63–69 cm

Call 'OOO-roo-oo'

Breeding Two eggs, 2–3 broods all year

Glossy, turquoise-green neck

Small wing bars

Broad tail band

♂

WOODPIGEON

The largest of all European pigeons, woodpigeons are commonly seen in gardens, parks, woodlands and around farms. Their feathers are mostly grey with a pinkish breast. As they have unusually dense, heavy feathers, they often appear almost round. These birds can be recognized when they walk by their distinctive waddle. Pigeons often eat seeds, but they will eat almost anything on a bird table.

SCALE

Most birds drink water by gulping it, then throwing their heads back, so the water pours down their throats. However pigeons suck water, using their beaks like straws.

FACT FILE

Scientific name
Columba palumbus

Size 40–42 cm

Wingspan 75–80 cm

Call Soft cooing

Breeding Two eggs in spring, can breed throughout the year

Bright yellow eyes

White-and-green bars on neck

Grey plumage on upperparts

Plump body

Narrow white bar visible on edge of wing

Short, red legs

♂

BARN OWL

Barn owls hunt for their food at night. Their bodies are covered in white-and-golden feathers. Like other owls, their eyes are on the front of their heads. They prefer open areas of land, but can be seen flying over gardens in the late evening as they search for prey. Barn owls make their homes in sheds, church spires and natural holes in trees.

SCALE

FACT FILE

Scientific name *Tyto alba*

Size 30–35 cm

Wingspan 90 cm

Call Screeching and hissing

Breeding 4–7 eggs, from April to May

Barn owls live alone or in pairs. Males and females usually mate for life and both parents look after the chicks. They are rare, and their nests must not be disturbed.

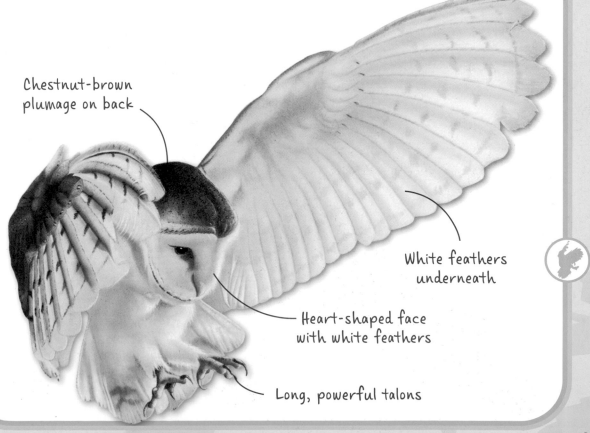

Chestnut-brown plumage on back

White feathers underneath

Heart-shaped face with white feathers

Long, powerful talons

SPARROWHAWK

Sparrowhawks are native residents, and are becoming more common around Britain following a severe drop in numbers caused by pesticide poisoning. The female is larger than the male, has brown upperparts and a white stripe over the eye. These birds of prey have rounded wings and long tails that are perfect for fast flight and weaving in and out of trees. Sparrowhawks do not hover.

SCALE

Sparrowhawks fly at speeds of up to 50 km/h, and need to get close to their prey before reaching out with their powerful talons.

FACT FILE

Scientific name *Accipiter nisus*

Size 28–40 cm

Wingspan 60–80 cm

Call 'Kekek' followed by 'peee'

Breeding 4–5 eggs are laid in one brood from March to June

Small, rounded head

Yellow eye

Greyish-brown plumage

Barred breast

Rounded wings

Yellow legs

Long tail

♂

TAWNY OWL

The tawny owl is a woodland predator that also lives in parks and gardens. These nocturnal birds normally hunt for small mammals, but they have moved into urban areas in search of small birds that gather around bird tables. Like other owls, they fly in eerie silence, their wing beats muffled by the downy edges of their wing feathers. As well as mammals and birds, tawny owls feed on insects, newts, frogs and bats.

SCALE

Tawny owls can look behind by twisting their heads around. They can pinpoint sound accurately by moving their heads to get a 'fix' on the source of the noise.

FACT FILE

Scientific name *Strix aluco*

Size 37–39 cm

Wingspan 94–104 cm

Call Hooting 'hoo-hoo' or 'ke-wik'

Breeding 2–5 eggs are laid in a single brood from April to June

Mottled, brown feathers

Large round head with distinctive facial disc and dark eyes

Paler colouring on underside

GLOSSARY

Bar A striped marking across a bird's feathers.

Breeding season The time of year when pairs of birds come together to breed and raise a family.

Brood A family of chicks.

Camouflage Colours, markings or patterns in a bird's feathers that help it to blend in with its surroundings and hide it from predators.

Carrion Dead or rotting animal flesh that is eaten by scavenging birds such as crows.

Clutch A group of eggs that are laid in one session and then incubated.

Cover Places where birds hide, such as bushes and hedges.

Eye-ring Pale-coloured feathers surrounding a bird's eye.

Facial disc A collection of feathers, especially noticeable on owls, that surrounds a bird's face and helps it to detect sound.

Fledgling A young bird that has recently grown its feathers.

Flock A group of birds feeding or travelling together.

Foliage A cluster of plant leaves, especially trees.

Forage To search extensively for food.

Forked The appearance of a bird's tail, split into a V-shape.

Habitat The natural home of an animal.

Incubate In birds, to sit on eggs to keep them warm so that the chicks will develop inside.

Migrant A bird that travels from one place to another at certain times of the year.

Migrate To travel from one place to another at certain times of the year. Many birds migrate between their winter and summer homes.

Nestling A bird that is too young to leave the nest.

Nocturnal Birds that are active at night instead of during the day.

Perch To stand or rest upon an object such as a branch.

Plumage The covering of feathers on a bird's body.

Predator An animal that hunts and eats other animals.

Prey An animal that is hunted and eaten by other animals.

Roost In birds, to rest or sleep.

Species A group of similar living things that breed together to produce young.

Talons The sharp, curved claws of raptors, such as sparrowhawks and owls.

Territory An area that a particular bird occupies and defends against other birds of the same species.